zero 제로	one 하나
two 두	three 세
four 네	five 다섯

six

육

seven

일곱

eight

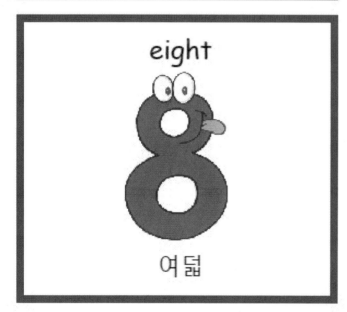

여덟

nine

아홉

ten

십

airplane

비행기

ball

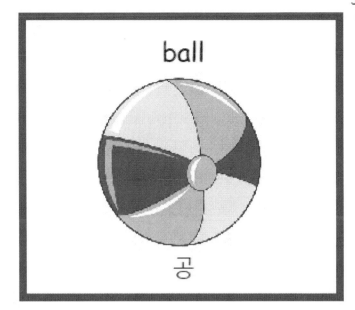

공

car

차

tame

길들인

scooter

스쿠터

flag

깃발

giraffe

기린

hand
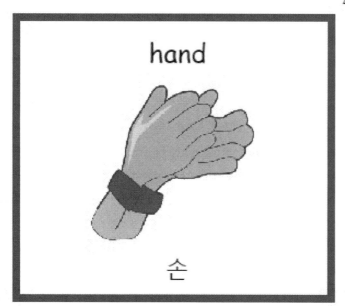
손

ice cream

아이스크림

jam

잼

kangaroo

캥거루

bug

곤충

monkey

원숭이

nap

선잠

octopus

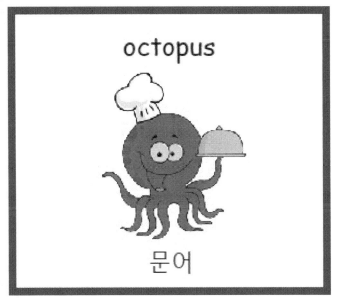

문어

pan

팬

celebrate

세상에 알리다

rabbit

토끼

shark

상어

tiger

호랑이

unicorn

일각수

vase

병 장식

watermelon

수박

towel

수건

yak

야크

zebra

얼룩말

alligator

악어

bag

가방

cake

케이크

dog

개

fall

가을

hedgehog

고습도치

igloo

이글루

jug

조끼

backpack

배낭

moon

달

nest

둥지

orange

주황색

parrot

앵무새

question

의문

animals

동물

sheep

양

tree

나무

umbrella

우산

volcano

화산

worm

벌레

anchor

앵커

yarn

방사

zipper

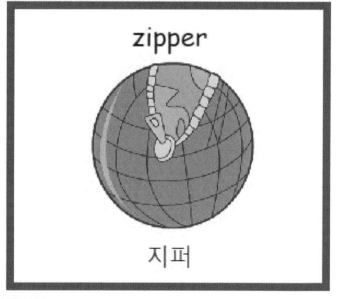

지퍼

ant

개미

baby

아가

cat

고양이

deer

사슴

elephant

코끼리

fish

물고기

groundhog

마개

hen

암탉

iguana

이구아나

jump

도약

king

왕

lion

사자

mole

몰

collar

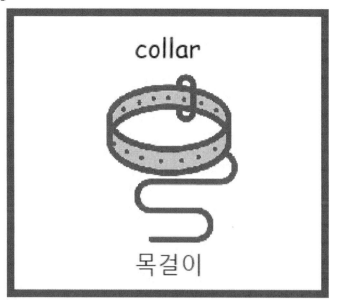

목걸이

owl

올빼미

pig

돼지

quilt

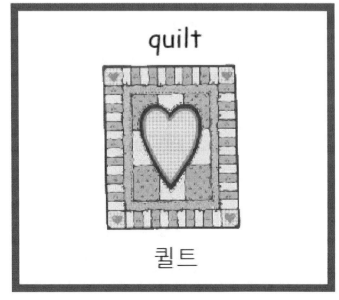

퀼트

rooster

수탉

snail

달팽이

turkey

터키

mirror

거울

violin

바이올린

whale

고래

shovel

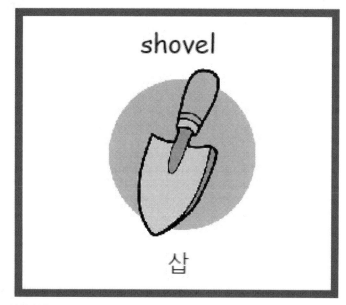

삽

yogurt

요거트

wreath

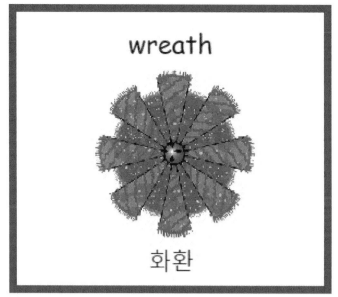

화환

bee

벌

duck

오리

tea

차

gorilla

고릴라

hill

언덕

ice

얼음

knife
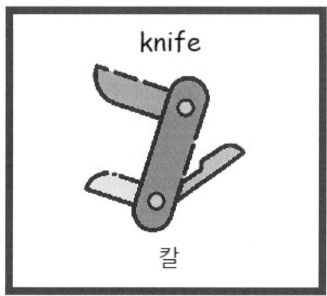
칼

kids

아이들

lemon

레몬

milk

우유

night

밤

pear

배

queen

퀸

ring

반지

socks

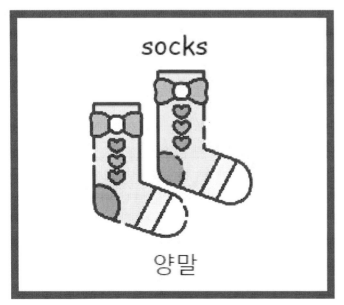

양말

water

물

kitchen

부엌

apple

사과

hello

HI!

여보세요

bear

곰

bed

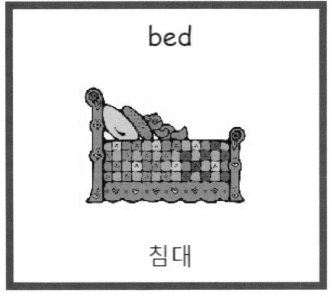

침대

bell

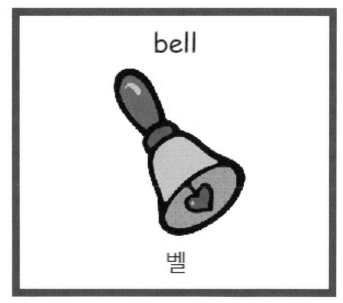

벨

bird

새

slippers

슬리퍼

boat

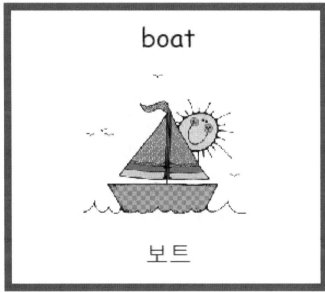

보트

box

상자

boy

소년

bread

빵

brother

동료

chair

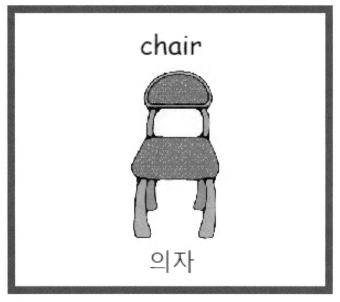

의자

chicken

치킨

children

어린이

christmas

크리스마스

coat

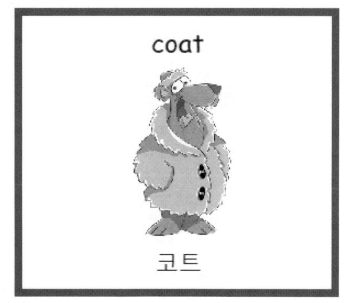

코트

corn

옥수수

cow

소

day

일

doll

인형

door

문

eyes

눈

farm

농장

farmer

농장주

father

아버지

fire

불

crab

게

flower

꽃

game

계략

garden

정원

girl

소녀

goodbye

안녕

grass

잔디

ground

바닥

head

머리

bookshelf

책장

horse

말

house

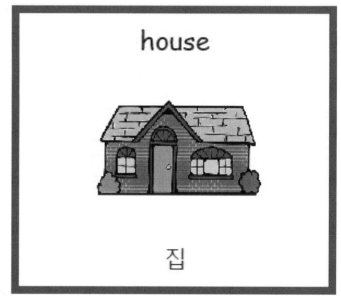

집

kitten

고양이 새끼

leg

다리

letter

편지

man

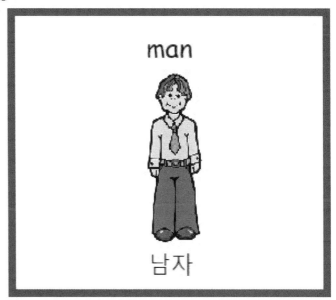

남자

oven

오븐

money

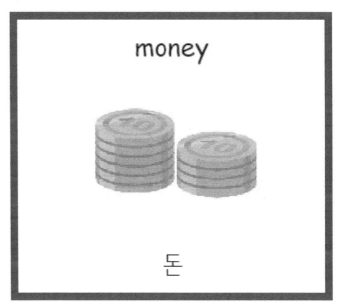

돈

morning

아침

mother

어머니

name

이름

paper

종이

party

파티

picture

그림

rain

비

witch

마녀

bottle

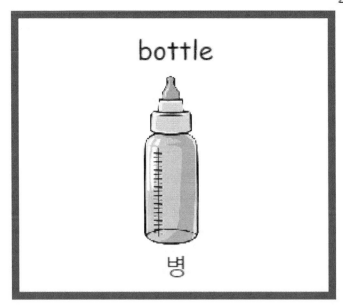

병

school

학교

seeds

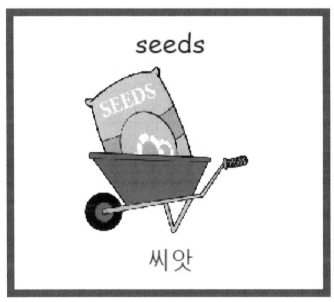

씨앗

shoes

구두

sister

여자 형제

snow

눈

song

노래

squirrel

다람쥐

stick

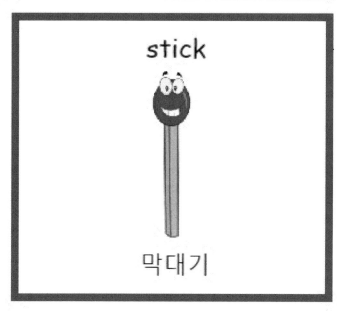

막대기

street

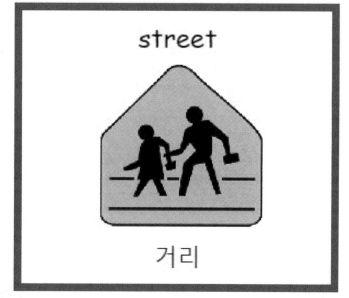

거리

sun

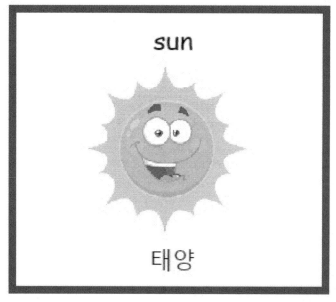

태양

lamp

램프

basketball

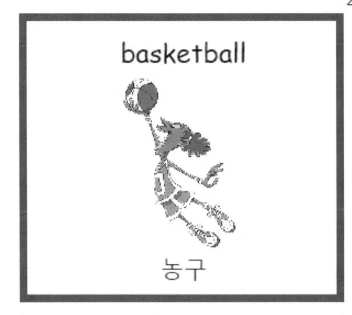

농구

cactus

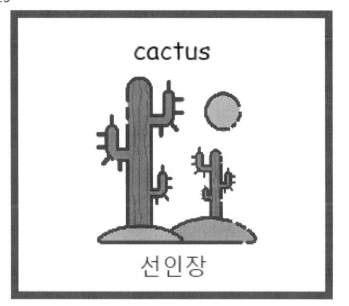

선인장

radio

라디오

toy

장난감

camera

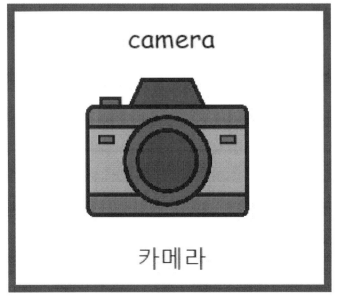

카메라

hammer

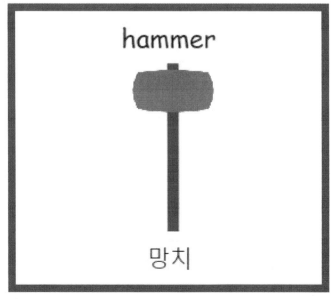

망치

wind

바람

window

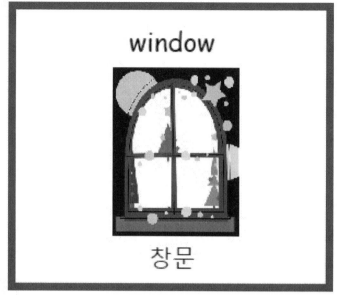

창문

wood

나무

butterfly

나비

camel

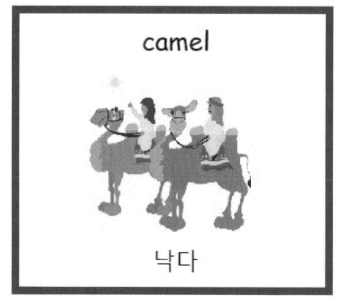

낙다

message

메시지

dolphin

돌고래

eagle

독수리

chick

병아리

fox

여우

frog

개구리

goat

염소

hippopotamus

하마

bicycle

자전거

dumbbells

덤벨

panda

팬더

puppy

강아지

mice

쥐

penguin

펭귄

snake

뱀

spider
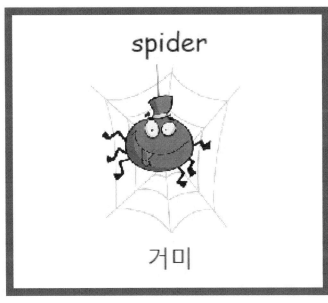
거미

turtle

터틀

wolf

늑대

sleeping

자고있는

plane

평면

parachute

낙하산

barber

이발사

friend

친구

coconut

코코넛

broccoli

브로콜리

gifts

선물

play

놀이

van

봉고차

comb

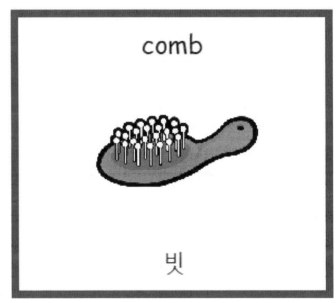

빗

gun

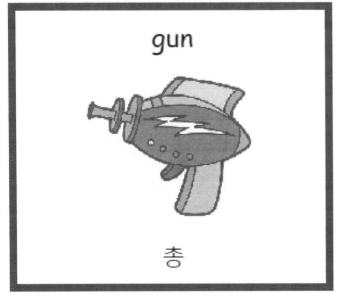

총

paintbrush

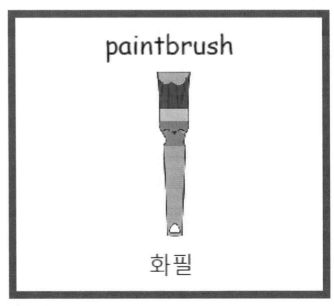

화필

peas

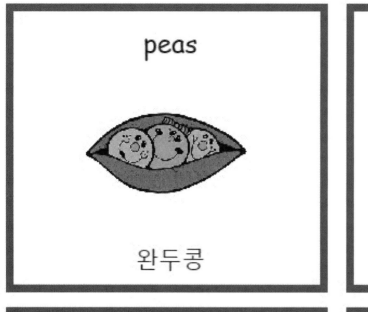

완두콩

ballon

풍선

baseball

야구

reading

독서

run

운영

book

책

shopping

쇼핑

showering

샤워

walk

산책

wash

빨래

earth
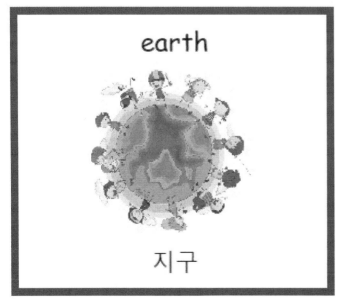
지구

happy

행복

salad

샐러드

sad

슬퍼

win

승리

cooking

조리

singing

명음

eat

먹다

cry

울음 소리

toilet

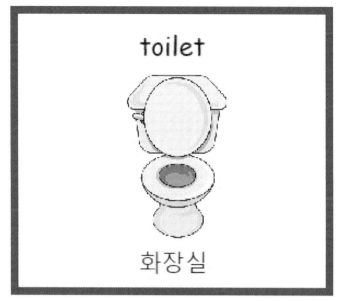

화장실

teach

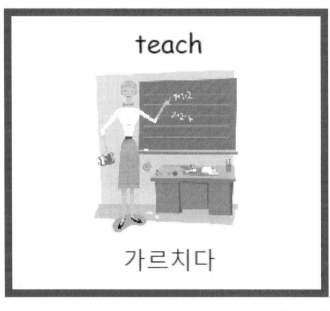

가르치다

drink

음주

writing

쓰기

bouquet

꽃다발

clean

깨끗한

hurt

상처

drawing

그림

bus

버스

laugh

웃음

bedroom

침실

pillow

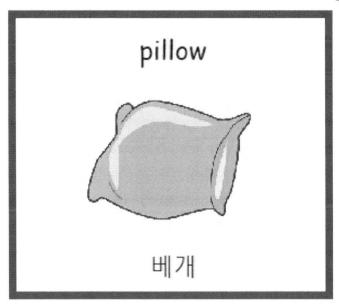

베개

sleepy

졸리는

wake up

일어나

working

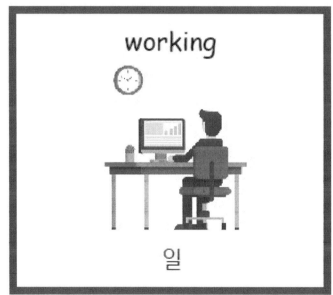

일

presents

선물

piano

피아노

tuxedo

턱시도

medicine

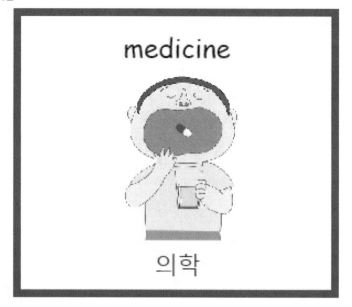

의학

climbing

등반

bone

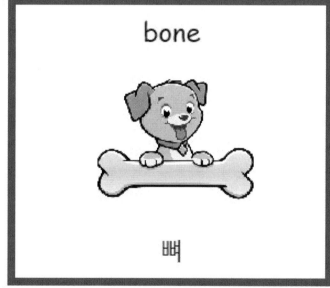

뼈

riding

승마

swimming

수영

dressing

드레싱

drum

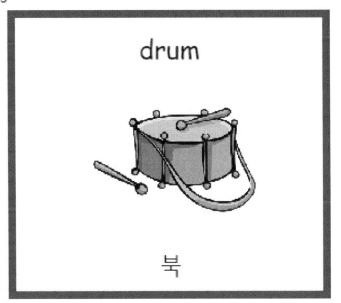

북

chili

칠리

suitcase

여행 가방

doctor

의사

hug

포옹

English Korean

math

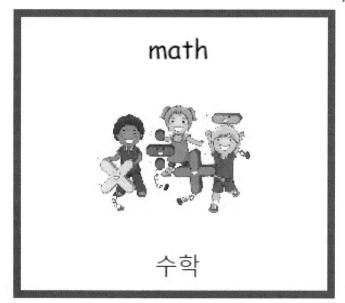

수학

soccer

축구

love

애정

ironing

다리미질

sick

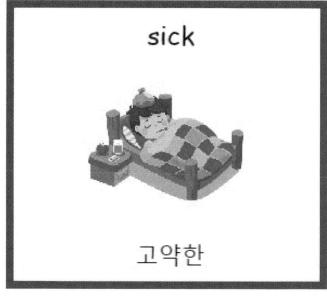

고약한

hair

머리

fireplace

난로

bike

자전거

cherry

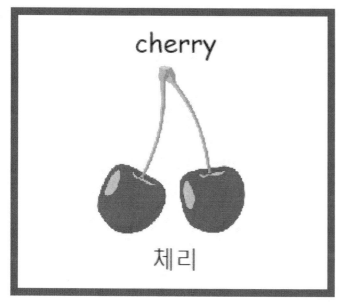

체리

banana

바나나

train

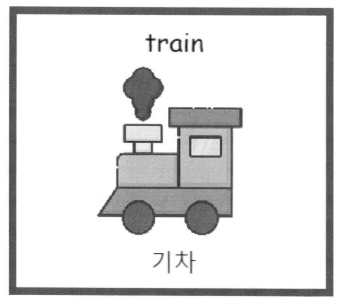

기차

truck

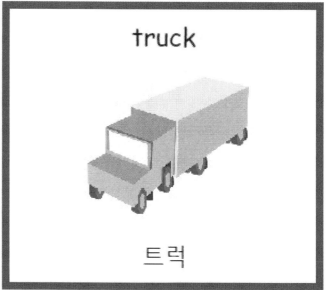

트럭

strawberry

딸기

pineapple

파인애플

ax

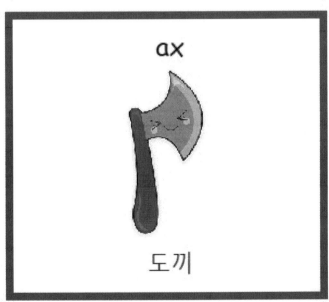

도끼

bean

콩

candy

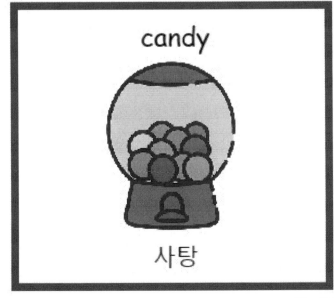

사탕

carpet

양탄자

dock
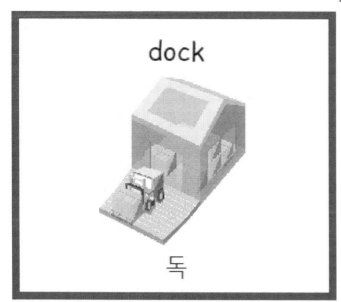
독

ears

귀

hotel
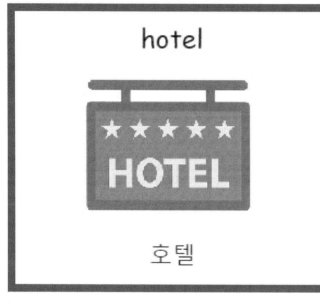
호텔

finger
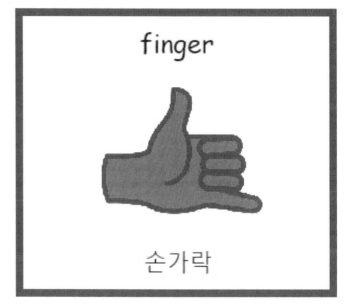
손가락

fly
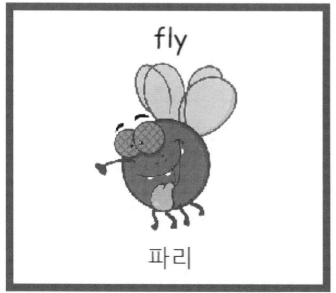
파리

ham

햄

English Korean

hat

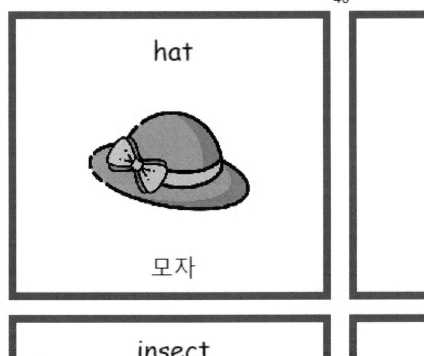

모자

impress

날인

insect

곤충

island

섬

juice

주스

jogging

조깅

kite

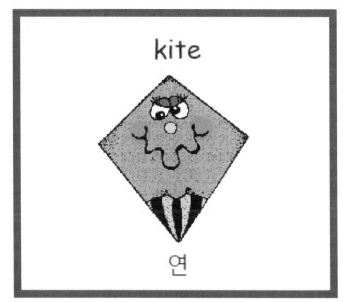

연

kiwi

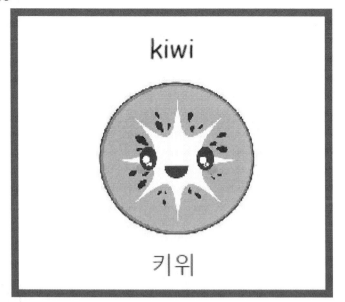

키위

koala

코알라

ladder

사닥다리

leaf

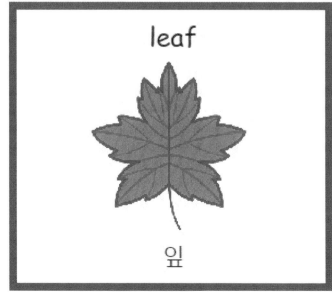

잎

angry

성난

meat

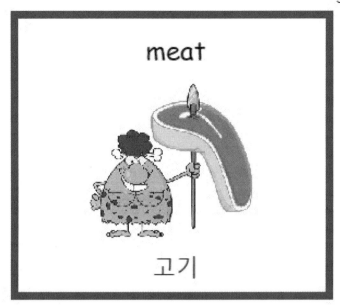

고기

nose

코

nurse

간호사

nut

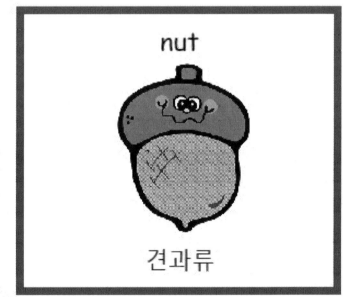

견과류

onion

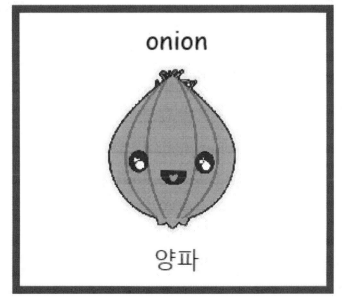

양파

oval

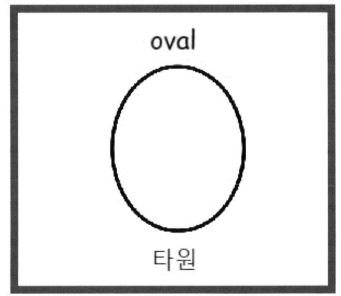

타원

palm

야자수

pen

펜

quail

메추라기

quiz

놀리다

rat

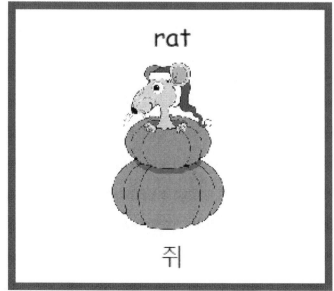

쥐

rocks

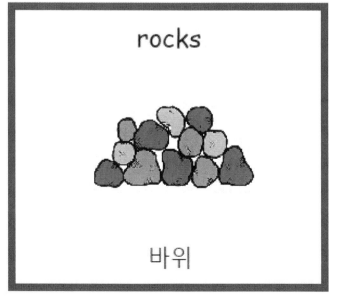

바위

ruler

지배자

skirt

치마

skunk

스컹크

star

별

tail

꼬리

tooth

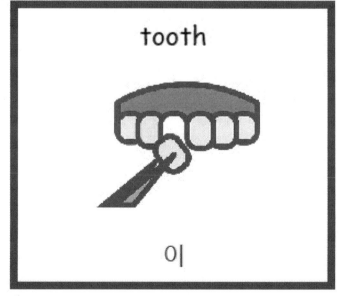

이

up

쪽으로

unhappy

불행한

under

아래에

vest

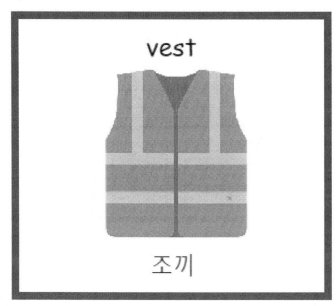

조끼

vaccine

백신

whiskey

위스키

turban

터번

ketchup

케첩

stove

난로

thunder

우뢰

jeep

지프

cheetah

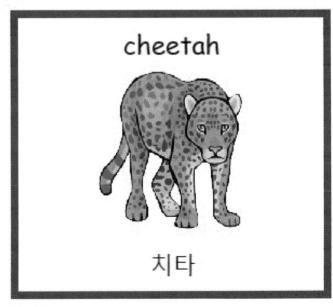

치타

English Korean

delivery

배달

magician

마술사

photographer

사진 작가

studying

공부하는

alphabet

알파벳

number

번호

coffee

커피

shoulder

어깨

clock

시계

lizard

도마뱀

spatula

주걱

fin

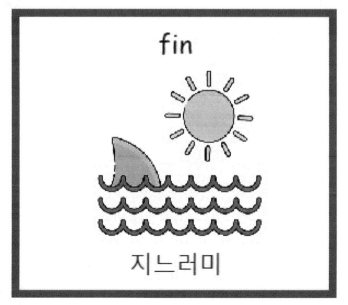

지느러미

torch

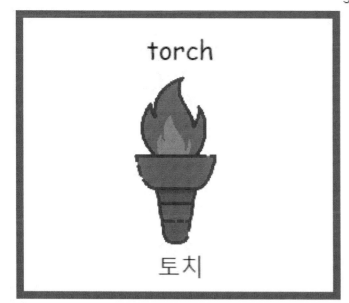

토치

lotus

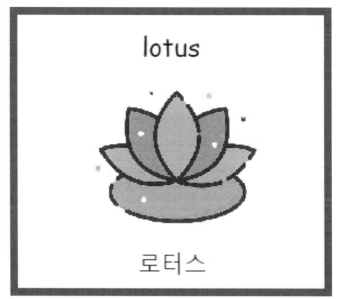

로터스

bowl

사발

pirate

해적

factory

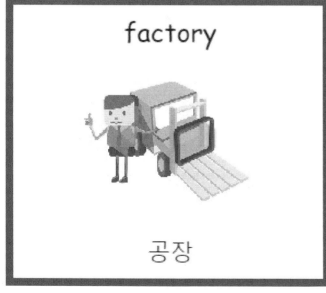

공장

pacifier

젖꼭지

helmet

헬멧

puddle

흐리게 하다

glove

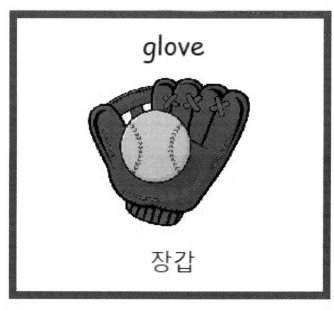

장갑

sailboat

요트

feeding

급송

pencil

연필

calendar

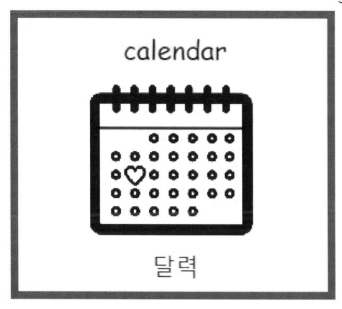

달력

tire

타이어

popsicles

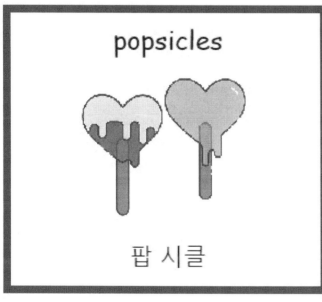

팝 시클

chimney

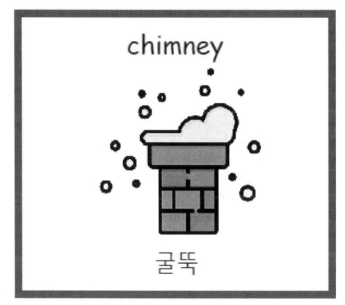

굴뚝

snowflake

눈송이

cheese

치즈

package

꾸러미

shy

수줍은

team

팀

sofa

소파

grape

포도

crayons

크레용

ink

잉크

glass

안경

curtain

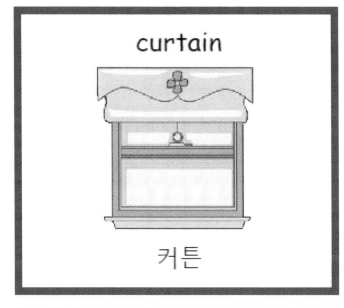

커튼

golf

골프

boxing

권투

cab

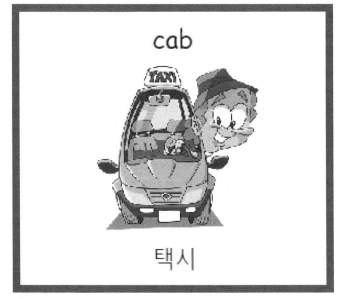

택시

hexagon

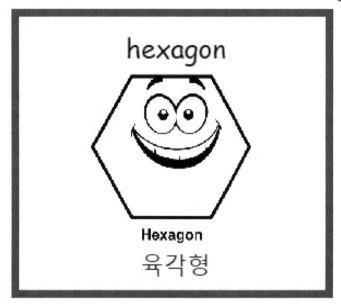

Hexagon

육각형

mare

바다

carrot

당근

belt

벨트

sweater

스웨터

compass

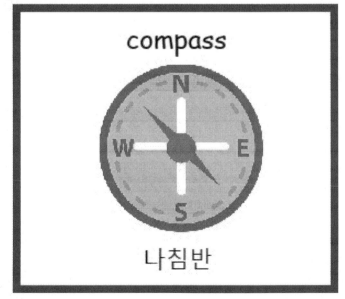

나침반

pudding

푸딩

rose
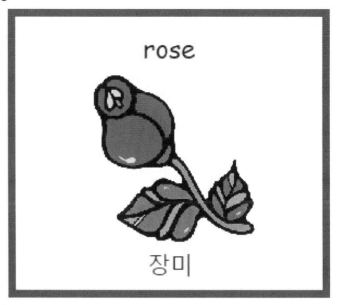
장미

dress

드레스

chef

요리사

jacket

재킷

summer

여름

angel

천사

knight

기사

broom

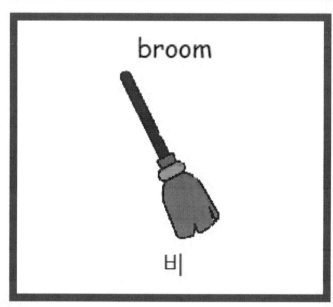

비

smelling

냄새

pajamas

잠옷

boots

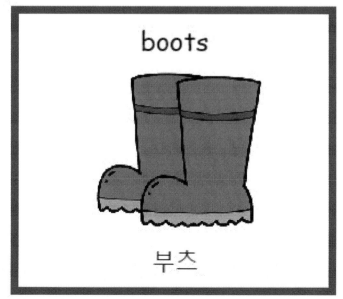

부츠

noodles

국수

lantern

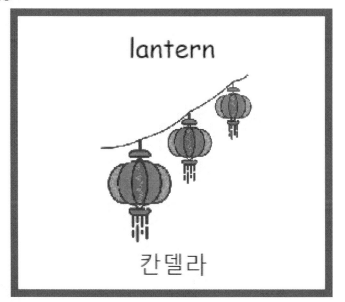

칸델라

scarf

스카프

shirt

셔츠

peanut

땅콩

shorts

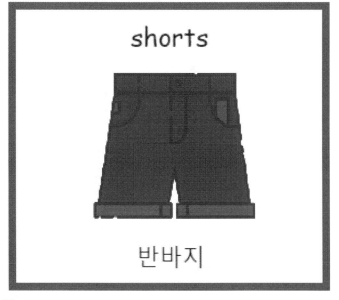

반바지

briefcase

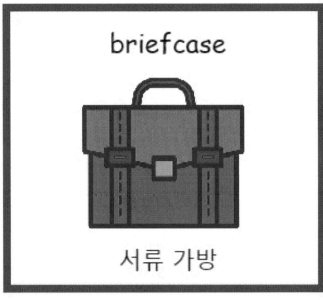

서류 가방

pagoda

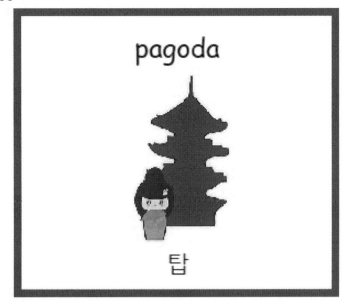

탑

stockings

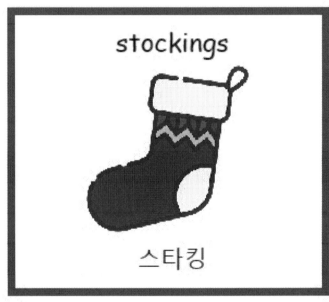

스타킹

syringe

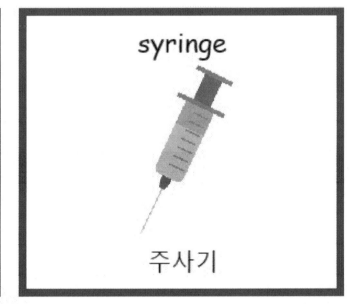

주사기

arm

팔

beard

수염

blood
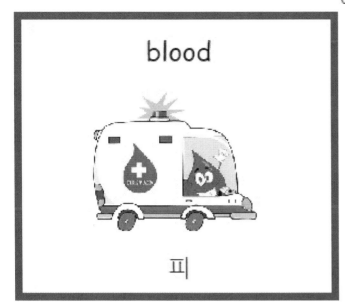
피

rainbow

무지개

microscope

현미경

mermaid

인어

scissors
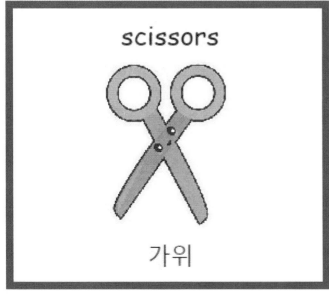
가위

chin

턱

potato

감자

elbow

팔꿈치

face

얼굴들

cutter

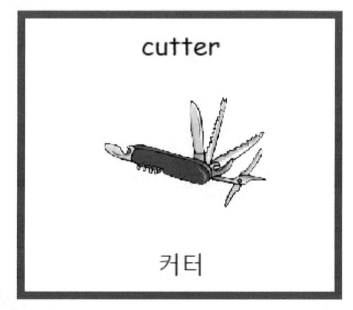

커터

medication

약물 치료

lipstick

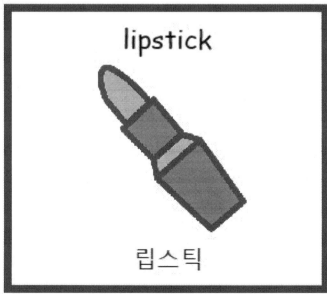

립스틱

driving

운전

windmill

풍차 비슷한 것

beach

바닷가

telescope

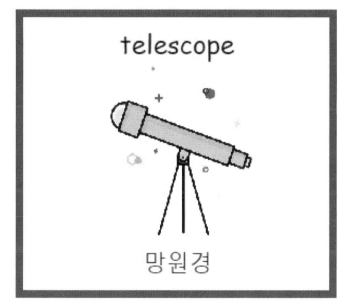

망원경

utensils

식기

tent

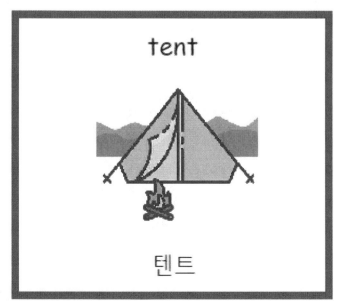

텐트

mouth

입

necklace

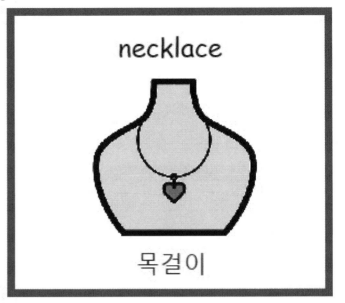

목걸이

neck

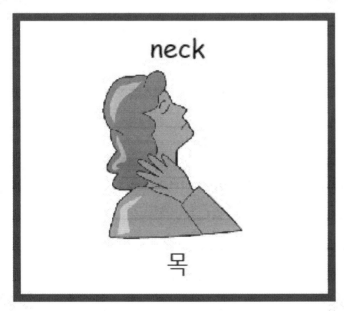

목

princess

공주님

pearls

진주

bomb

폭탄

teeth

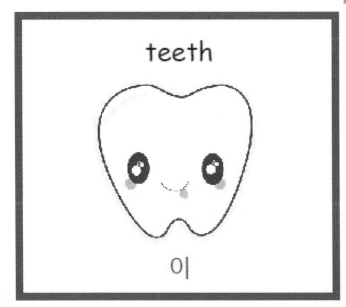

이

steak

스테이크

donut

도넛

thumb

무지

dice

주사위

news

뉴스

tongue

혀

glue

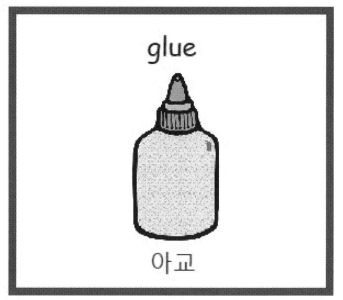

아교

wagon

왜건

rocket

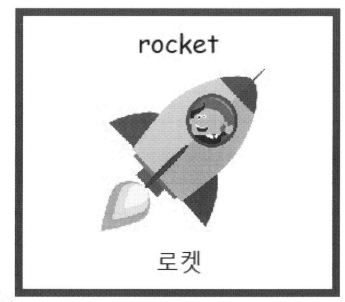

로켓

ostrich

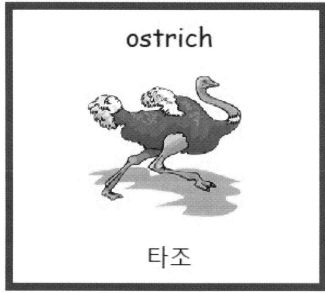

타조

teapot

주전자

oyster

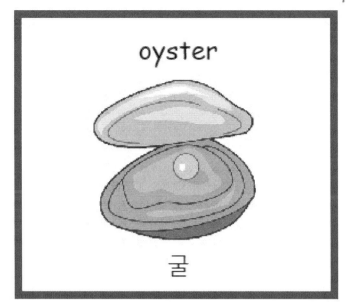

굴

pelican

펠리컨

pigeon

비둘기

porcupine

호저

reindeer

순록

vegetable

야채

sausage

소시지

pie

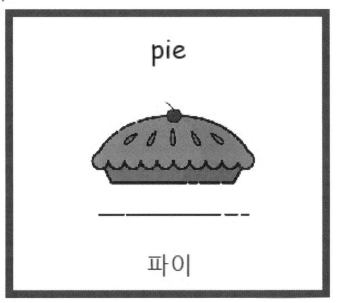

파이

honey

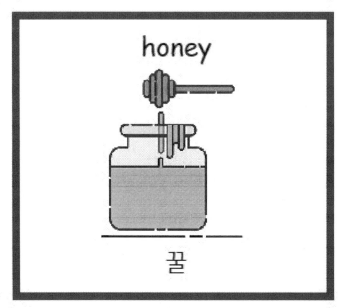

꿀

blender

믹서기

swan

백조

toad

두꺼비

vulture

대머리수리

walrus

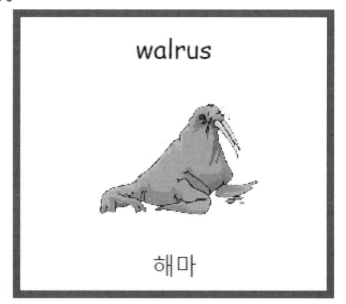

해마

soup

수프

avocado

아보카도

chocolate

초콜릿

pizza

피자

tomato

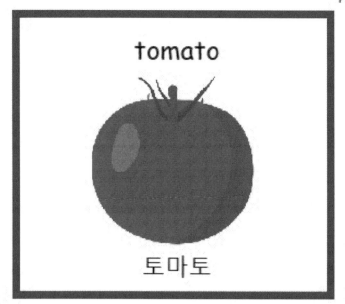

토마토

eggplant

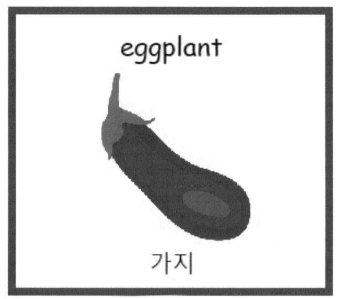

가지

cucumber

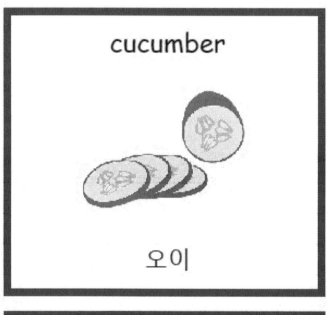

오이

grapefruit

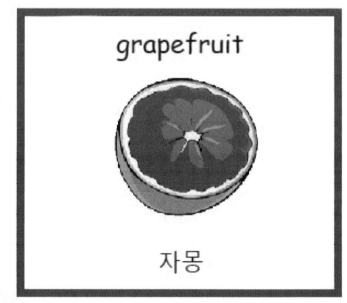

자몽

calculator

계산자

museum

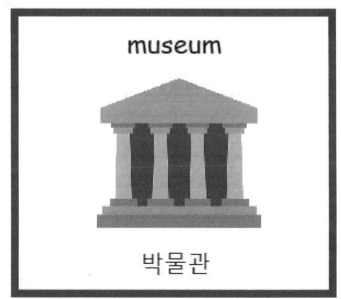

박물관

teacher

선생

sandwich

샌드위치

muscle

근육

peach

복숭아

egg

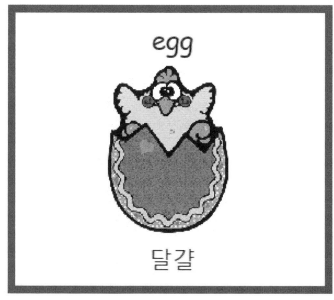

달걀

plum

자두

English Korean

pomegranate

석류 나무

serving

피복재

raspberry

산딸기

tangerine

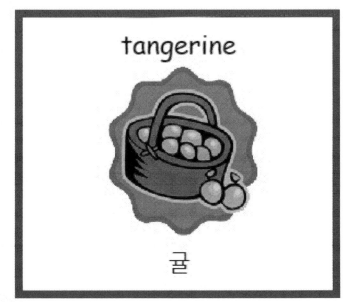

귤

bad

나쁜

dad

아빠

joyful

즐거운

stand up

일어서 다

mad

미친

podium

지휘대

friendly

친한

proud

교만한

decrease

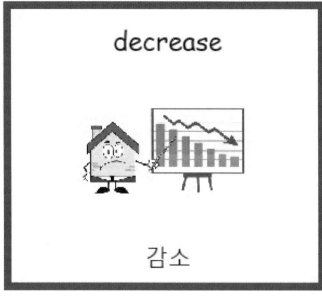

감소

lightbulb

전구

wiping

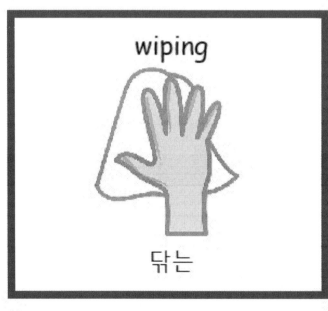

닦는

sinking

가라 앉는

castle

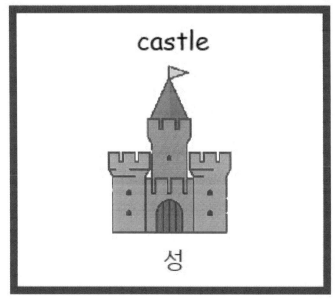

성

wag

흔들기

forbid

금지 된

open

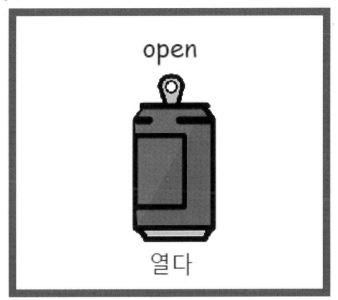

열다

artist

예술가

race

경주

wallet

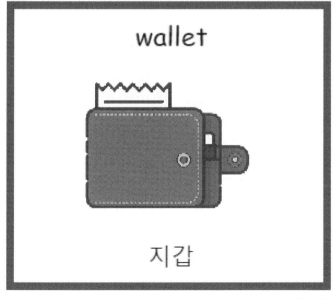

지갑

bored

지루한

kneeling

무릎 꿇는

map

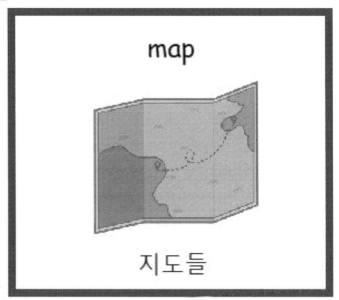

지도들

hockey

하키

powerful

강한

hospital

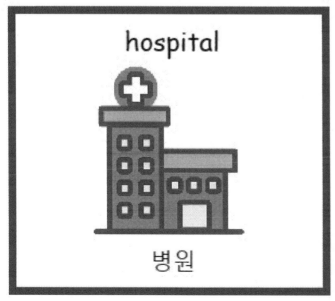

병원

clam

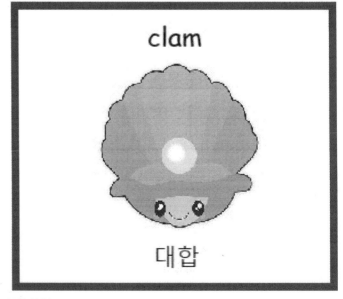

대합

fat

지방

mat

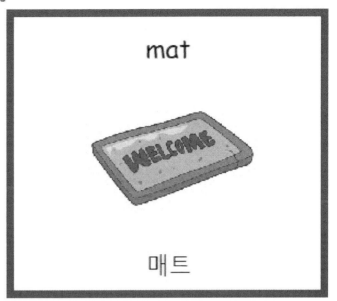

매트

clap

박수

teacup

찻잔

mountains

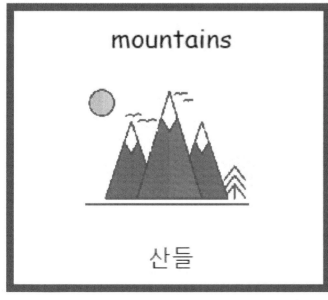

산들

science

과학

knitting

편물

musician

음악가

gasoline

가솔린

butcher

푸주한

leader

지도자들

red

빨간

Made in the USA
San Bernardino, CA
26 November 2019